Merry Christmas to

Dad from Kathy & Bob

Washington, 1977

One Man's Fancy

ONE MAN'S FANCY

CHARLES SAXON

DODD, MEAD & COMPANY • NEW YORK

1   2   3   4   5   6   7   8   9   10

The artist wishes to thank Barbara Nicholls of the Nicholls Gallery
for her help and cooperation, and *Town & Country*, *The New York
Times*, *Woman's Day*, and The New England Merchants Bank for
permission to use those drawings of his for which they hold the
copyright.

Of the 157 drawings in this book, 139 appeared originally in *The New
Yorker* and were copyrighted © in the years 1962 through 1977,
inclusive, by The New Yorker Magazine, Inc.

Library of Congress Cataloging in Publication Data

Saxon, Charles D
One man's fancy.

1. American wit and humor, Pictorial. I. Title.
NC1429.S35A52   741.5'973   77-11737
ISBN 0-396-07509-6

*For Akiko
and the future*

"*Lucille, do we kiss the Friedlanders?*"

"I'm fifty-seven years old, but with the wind-chill factor I feel eighty-three."

Gallery Opening

"I'm very sorry, Freddie, but I'm afraid I just don't relate to potted plants."

"I said I like it. Period. I no longer feel I need to lie to spare your feelings."

"Remember, Stuart. Love conquers all."

"Ladybugs did that? I always thought they were good bugs!"

"It was *nice*. *Hard times give everyone such a sense of camaraderie.*"

"*Would you welcome Mr. and Mrs. Edgar Garfield.*"

"*Tell me, Norman, does anyone ever ask you what I'm really like?*"

"*That's Dolores Granger.
She gave up everything for love.*"

"*Steer clear of that one. Every day is always the first day of the rest of his life.*"

"*So you're a cellist! You know, I don't think I've ever seen a cellist without a cello.*"

"*I hate these one-man shows.*"

"What did you learn in school today?"

"I feel I should warn you. They've taken down most of Boston and they're putting up something else."

BOSTON

"Our first mistake was letting go of the town meeting."

"*It's awful! Ever since I started using my mind again, I just can't stop!*"

"We enjoyed your lecture so much. But isn't there some way of telling youth we don't resent them for being what they are so they won't resent us for being establishment?"

"Now, they *look like* nice people."

"*All I said was, when we were girls we strolled these paths and sang little French songs in unison.*"

"*I tell you it is, Francis! It's the Codman crest!*"

"Whiskey and water, Tommy-
boy. Charge it to the Family
Trust."

"Couldn't we break our rule about hitchhikers just this once?"

"*I never can remember. Is it Manet or Monet who isn't as good as the other?*"

"Considering your route and the length of time you'll be away, I'm sure you'll want to protect your loved ones with our blanket coverage that includes storms at sea, shipwreck, demons of both the land and the deep, sirens and monsters, in addition to all acts of the gods."

"Louis, I want you to know Mr. Pickett, one of my oldest and dearest friends."

Of late, Arnold Flagler had begun to spend much of his weekend time walking alone in the woods. One day, he found himself on an unfamiliar path that led him to a small pond.

As he stood beside the pond, the water began to stir and bubbles to rise

until they formed a lovely little fountain, and a voice called, "Arnold Flagler, this is the fountain of youth!"

THE FOUNTAIN OF YOUTH

Mr. Flagler shrank back in fear. The fountain leaped and soared, and a sound of unbelievable music filled the air.

The voice called again. "This is the fountain of youth, Arnold Flagler! Drink!"

"What will happen to me if I drink?" Mr. Flagler asked.

"Youth will be yours," said the fountain.

"I mean, how does it work? How young will I be?" The fountain swirled and sang as it danced higher and higher. "Youth will be yours," it repeated.

"Will my family know me? What about my pension and the cumulative profit-sharing plan, and all that?"
The voice of the fountain was fainter now.
"Youth will be yours," it said.

"Listen," said Mr. Flagler desperately. "Just tell me one thing. Has anybody else tried this? Anybody I know?"
The music faded away and the water subsided until the fountain vanished and the pond was still.

"What did you do in the woods today?" asked his wife that evening.
"I got lost," said Mr. Flagler.

Mr. Flagler walked slowly home.

"How do we know he isn't just trying to make damn fools of us?"

"Say, Frank, did I leave some boughs of holly and a little Christmas tree in here last night?"

"Emily! For the love of God!"

"So! Mr. Board of Zoning!
Our paths cross again!"

"During his latter years, Mr. Hoyt spent most of his time
watching television."

"Is something troubling you, Bennet? I've never known you to chew gum."

"Well, so long. See you next September."

"*I think you just missed something. The ball went up in the air and somebody caught it and the crowd's yelling like mad.*"

"*Dear, you remember Mrs. Leeming.
We met way back during Civil Rights.*"

"*For heaven's sake! Get a grip on yourself and go to sleep!*"

"*Do you call* this *Kushi-Katsu?*"

"No, I am not interested in knowing how you would rate me on a scale of one to ten."

"*You don't think it's too Christmassy?*"

"I'm beginning to think everybody in the whole world is
preoccupied with sex except Henry and me."

"Now tell me, Mr. Hilbert, does Merrill Lynch think utilities are going to keep on being iffy?"

"Shouldn't someone be speaking out about that?"

"Do you mind? I'm forming an opinion!"

"I'm not just sitting here. I'm listening to Johann Sebastian Bach."

"Now he does a little dance, and then she won't be mad."

"It seems to me that you've simply got to be for or against sex these days."

"Poor Mr. Plummer keeps losing his conversation group."

"Did someone in here buzz?"

Awareness of Man as a Living Machine

Denial of Apathy

Decline of Puritanism

Nostalgia for the Natural Man

SOME ASPECTS OF THE EMERGING
AMERICAN CHARACTER

Tolerance of New Art Forms

Involvement

Tendency to Polarization

"*I declare, sometimes I think our whole life is arranged for tax purposes.*"

"*You needn't tell me what they are, Norris, but have you any secrets you plan to carry with you to the grave?*"

"*Jonathan, when did you start saying 'Mark my words'?*"

"Sheldon, why don't you
ever leap up?"

"Tell me again what my mental attitude
should be for a bunker shot."

"If there are any calls, Miss Gilmore, I'll be on the fifteenth floor, breathing down some necks."

"Of course you have a pretty smile. Would I have married a woman with an ugly smile?"

PARIS

"Isn't it lovely to get back to Maxim's? It's almost like being home at '21.'"

"Can't you relax and sip like everybody else and let the boulevard speak to you?"

"Good God! I barely made it with the mini the last time around."

"*This gentleman says he'd be delighted to show us where Fitzgerald and Hemingway used to go.*"

"*Have you noticed, Luanne, that Paris is full of foreigners?*"

"We have a little vineyard of our own
back in Bakersfield, California."

"You're the one who
wanted to buy oranges and
croissants—you *carry*
them past the concierge."

"A little Braque would be a perfect memento; n'est-ce pas, Paxton?"

"How can all these people afford it?"

"*You know how it is, Ted. Since I went to Princeton, I was sort of hoping you'd want to go somewhere else.*"

"*I'd like to make it clear that I am not speaking for my generation. I am speaking for your mother and myself.*"

"*Leonard, what do my clothes say about me?*"

"*He keeps flying off in the dead of night to places like South Africa and Kuala Lumpur, but it must be all right, because he's with Standard Oil.*"

"*Brian, this is Lars Kronquist. He's a winner, too.*"

"No, we can't play paddle tennis. We can't play anything. Richard is going to finish 'The Decline and Fall of the Roman Empire' if it kills him."

"*I thought pheasants didn't begin until October.*"

"*Are you going to believe me or some encyclopedia you picked up in a supermarket?*"

"*This is between you and me, Constance. Let's leave the Republican Party out of it!*"

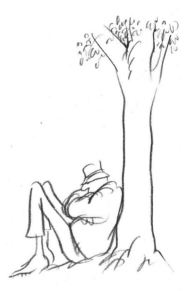

"*The Rites of Spring probably aren't getting any duller. Maybe we're just getting older.*"

"Everybody back in twenty minutes or we'll miss tea at the pub near the place where Bill Sikes murdered Nancy."

"May I say 'Travis and I were enthralled by Hatfield House'?"

COME TO BRITAIN

"He says Chizzik is Chiswick."

"After the rains, the elves and wee folk come out to dance in the meadow by the ancient abbey."

"I just bought everybody silver mustard pots."

"We've got to be getting back. Herbert must have his pint of bitter before dinner."

"I'm absolutely exhausted, and we've still got Scotland to face."

"The less said about this young lady the better. When her husband, the second Earl, was away at the wars, her conduct left something to be desired, if we can believe the gossip of the period."

"We're a couple of Hoosiers from the States. Would you consider Woburn Abbey a must?"

"Two Irish coffees—with Sanka."

"You don't see one dirty window."

"Philip, 'Kojak' is starting."

"If you're off duty, why are you in front of Saks?"

"*Aren't you lucky! Very few people have anything original that's nice.*"

"When Henry Bigelow said, 'The sky is the daily bread of the eyes,' all you could come up with was 'Yes, it's always seemed that way to me, too.'"

"*My rival is the sea.*"

"*Thayer! Come quick! Wild raspberries!*"

"*Do you have any jolly fiction?*"

"Maybe clay isn't my thing."

"If you're just going to brood, why not try your
hand at some poetry?"

"*Here's a hot one. Some college wants to give you an honorary doctorate in humanities.*"

"*Pierce, of Bailey, Pierce & Kemp, may I present Archer, of Howe, Archer, Groff & Seaberry?*"

"Too much Christmas."

"Your family would like to know if you have slaked your thirst."

"Dear Aunt Frieda:
Thank you very much for the large book...."

"Greg, Jr., and I have great rapport."

"We were hoping you'd be home for vacation, or whatever
Moonies call it when they're not doing what they do."

"Oh, for goodness' sake! Smoke!"

"Your armies have deserted you, you have been wounded unto death.
Now make me feel it!"

"Listen to me, Francine! Stay in Wellesley! We can discuss who you are
and who I am over the vacations!"

"*Christopher has never been treated unkindly by adults. He trusts us implicitly. I hope, Miss Forbes, you won't in any way betray that trust.*"

"Gee! Everybody's going to the Museum of Natural History!"

"*Tell me again. What was it you liked about Walden?*"

"I grant your point, but not because I agree with you. I'm under sedation."

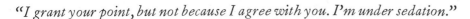

"What's my real motivation? Am I switching to convertible bonds because it's sensible or because waning self confidence is driving me from the common stocks into the relative security of convertible debentures?"

"Well, if everybody else is going to go berserk, I'll have a rum swizzle, too."

"*If you're looking for me, Herbert, I shall be sitting in the bay window reading the Dow Jones summary of corporate earnings.*"

"They don't look like wives."

"I'm learning to think not only with my mind, but with my entire body."

THE RACHMANINOFF FILE

First the strange mixup with the baggage and the prattle of the boorish Count Deschamps. Now customs was impounding his Beretta. Still, Holcomb Travis was determined to let nothing spoil his holiday.

The urgent summons to the cabaret proved to be a false alarm. But there was Gillian Lathrop. A delightful coincidence—or was it?

When the body of St. Alistair Royce was discovered sprawled between the neat rows of Chassagne-Montrachet, Herman Laubrich had already disappeared, to no one's surprise.

They were all there in the dining salon: Baron Rosenwasser, Herr Klimt, Mrs. Parsegian, and the Marburgs. As he studied the wine list, all the pieces seemed to fit into place.

Serge Katzourakis was followed everywhere by the obsequious Mr. Waxman. Were they actually father and son?

The usually taciturn Frau Berthe had been oddly insistent about changing his towels at precisely 11:25. Normally, she changed the Hochfelds' towels at 11:25.

If Prager had not bent forward at that moment to retrieve Professor Hensle's lighter, the runaway ski would have brought the pursuit to a grisly conclusion.

Inspector Forsythe observed that Dr. Kesselman had been asleep in the lounge when Mme. Fleischer was attacked, and also when the mail arrived. He was there still.

Just as the warning whistle blew, he became aware of two figures racing through the steam toward the Trans-Europe Express. Suddenly he knew the answer. But was it too late?

"*Margaret Spicer! After all these years! And you haven't changed a bit!*"

"Wouldn't it be nice if some large group came out for the status quo?"

"*I think I'm finally learning to live in the present.*"

"*Where's the foreground, do you think?*"

"*What am I supposed to say when you say, 'Eventide, the verdant woods among'?*"

"*It's okay if he bakes, or it's okay if he knits. But it's not okay if he bakes and knits.*"

ITALIA

" 'So let it be with Caesar. The noble
Brutus
Hath told you Caesar was ambitious.
If it were so it was a grievous fault,
And grievously hath Caesar answer'd it.
Here, under leave of Brutus . . .'"

"Over there are the Catacombs, and just beyond is the house of Gina Lollobrigida."

"Don't pester your mother. She's absorbing."

"*The Doges' Palace is* not *a tourist trap!*"

"*I don't want to see anything else. I'm out of film.*"

"*There are exactly one hundred and thirty-seven Spanish Steps.*"

"*When I get home, I'm going to paint, paint, paint!*"

"*Let me see . . . Why do I envy you? I envy you your taste, your roses, your husband.*"

"I couldn't find a thing on sale except convertible sofas."

"I don't know what's happening to my game! See
if you can tell me what I'm doing wrong."

"Hold it, Mr. Broadhurst!
The boy just delivered the 'Times'!"

"When did you start quoting 'Rolling Stone'?"

"Watch out for Archie Hopkins. He collects people."

"We brought along someone who needs no introduction."

"*I know! Let's play that adult game you got for Christmas.*"

"*We are about to make our first exploration of one of the most magical of all the arts. Inherent in those seemingly lifeless lumps of clay are forms only your minds can call forth. I have just one request before we begin: Please, no ashtrays.*"

"*I'm writing my autobiography, to set the record straight.*"

"*You know who I'm going to enjoy watching get older? Farrah Fawcett-Majors.*"

"*Oh dear, I forgot something to munch on.*"

Insomnia

"*The market gave a good account of itself today, Daddy, after some midmorning profit-taking.*"

"It's been done."

"I want to talk to you about the way you're frittering away your life."

"Oh, I know what you're going to say: 'You just don't understand.' Well, I understand this, my friend. You're headed down a dead-end street!"

"I'm talking about a sense of purpose. You've got to look for direction to find direction."

"I suppose it's my fault. What kind of example have I been, right? Well, I'm not ashamed of the modest success I've had with my materialistic orientation."

"O.K., so I suppose I'm wrong. Put down that paper and tell me how I've failed."

"*I'm listening. Would you like to finish any unfinished sentences?*"

"No 'Ban MIRV' sticker on the Mercedes, Arthur. If you insist, you can put it on the Plymouth."

"*Tell me, Wentworth. If you're not being inscrutable, just what are you being?*"

"The Kelleys, the Danvers, the Kornfelds, and the Rollinses all have tomatoes coming out of their ears."

"There's really not much to tell. I just grew up and married the girl next door."

"Walter, do we have a meaningful relationship?"

"On the other hand, isn't naturalness the greatest affectation?"

"*He certainly is not just a dog. He's my dog.*"

THE DAY THE TRAFFIC STOPPED

Wilfred Garber, driving a 1971 Plymouth Fury en route from a weekend in San Luis Obispo with his wife and three children, may have been the first to run out of gas. Other drivers in the vicinity of the Ventura turn-off say he was, but CBS-TV News reports it was a motorist near Topanga Canyon.

Helen Miller and her friend Debbie Lopez accepted the invitation to come and sit with two real cute boys in a Barris-customized Volkswagen behind them. Helen said it was all part of the conspiracy of the Power Structure and the Oil People. One of the boys said "right on, but you may never get back to Long Beach again." She said she didn't care any more.

Officer H.P. Edwards of the state highway patrol sat in his cruiser near Banning on the Palm Springs road. He told the first few people who asked that there wasn't a damn thing he could do. Then he locked up and climbed over the hill. He never looked back.

Mr. and Mrs. Donald Spicer were blocked in the parking lot at the Woodland Hills Shopping Center three and a half miles from home, where they had driven to pick up a quart of milk and some sliced pastrami. Mr. Spicer said "Don't give me that look. If you had remembered this stuff yesterday we could have been home watching all this on television."

Herb Arkwright just happened to have a can of Simoniz and some good rubbing cloths in the trunk. By nightfall he had his royal-blue Galaxie 500 glowing like a magazine ad.

Normally, Walter Fletcher could make the run from Palos Verdes to Westwood in 43 minutes on the San Diego Freeway. But he never made it beyond the L.A. County Airport.

Gary Schroeder telephoned his mother in Van Nuys to say he and Lulene and the kids would probably not get there for dinner. His mother asked him what she was supposed to do with a whole lamb in the oven. He said "The world is coming to an end," and she said, "Always on Sunday afternoon."

It was just past 9:30 when Tommy Kammerman's battery gave out and his stereo tape deck shuddered into silence. It was the last sound heard on the Santa Monica Freeway. The headlights were dimmed, air conditioners muffled, power windows immobilized. All was still.

"*We'd love to have you come for
a visit. And bring your little friend with you.*"

"*I found some old letters you wrote me before we were married.
Your handwriting has quite noticeably changed.*"

"*You bet your sweet life we're deductible. They're deductible when they're at our place.*"

"*I want you to promise me you'll give Bella Abzug one more chance to turn you on.*"

"*I had the strangest dream, Edgar. You were the only boy in the world and I was the only girl.*"

"Yoo-hoo! Fergusons! Remember us? Camelback Inn—six no trump doubled."

"During your formative years, I worked hard to create the proper father image for you. Now I think it's time you got to meet the man behind that image."

"Let him speak now or forever hold his peace."

"*Apartment 6-B, 310 West Sixty-eighth Street, New York. Zip Code 10023. 212-695-9445.*"

"Now that you're retiring, you won't be renewing this 'Insider's Newsletter,' I assume."

"Do you know what your generation will see, young fellow? Your generation will see Dow-Jones industrials break through the two-thousand level."